Marie Antoinette

Jane Bingham

South Huntington Pub. Lib.
145 Pidgeon Hill Rd.
Huntington Sta., N.Y. 11746

Chicago, Illinois

 **HEINEMANN-RAINTREE**

TO ORDER:
- Phone Customer Service **888-454-2279**
- Visit **www.heinemannraintree.com** to browse our catalog and order online.

© 2009 Raintree
a division of Pearson Inc.
Chicago, Illinois

All rights reserved. No part of this publication may be reproduced or transmitted in any form or by any means, electronic or mechanical, including photocopying, recording, taping, or any information storage and retrieval system, without permission in writing from the publisher.

Editorial: Louise Galpine, Diyan Leake, and Kristen Truhlar
Design: Jennifer Lacki, Kim Miracle, and Betsy Wernert
Illustrations: Mapping Specialists
Picture Research: Mica Brancic
Production: Vicki Fitzgerald

Originated by Modern Age
Printed and bound in China by Leo Paper Group

ISBN-13: 978-1-4109-3220-4 (hc)
ISBN-10: 1-4109-3220-6 (hc)

12 11 10 09 08
10 9 8 7 6 5 4 3 2 1

Library of Congress Cataloging-in-Publication Data
Bingham, Jane.
  Marie Antoinette / Jane Bingham.
     p. cm. -- (Great women leaders)
  Includes bibliographical references and index.
  ISBN 978-1-4109-3220-4 (hc)
  1. Marie Antoinette, Queen, consort of Louis XVI, King of France, 1755-1793--Juvenile literature. 2. Queens--France--Biography--Juvenile literature. 3. France--History--Louis XVI, 1774-1793--Juvenile literature. I. Title.
  DC137.1.B59 2008
  944'.035092--dc22
  [B]
                                                  2007049816

Acknowledgments
The publishers would like to thank the following for permission to reproduce photographs: © akg-images **pp. 13** (Erich Lessing), **16** (Jerume da Cunha), **26, 31**; ©Alamy (Visual Arts Library, London) **p. 37**; ©The Art Archive **pp. 7** (Museum der Stadt Wien/Dagli Orti), **25** (Dagli Orti), **27** (Musee du Chateau de Versailles/Dagli Orti), **32** (Marc Charmet), **33** (Marc Charmet), **40** (Bibliotheque des Arts Decoratifs Paris/Gianni Dagli Orti); ©The Bridgeman Art Library **pp. 4** (Chateau de Versailles, France/ Giraudon/Lauros), **6** (Private Collection/Photo ©Christie's Images), **8** (Chateau de Versailles), **9** (Kunsthistorisches Museum, Vienna, Austria), **10** (Schloss Schonbrunn, Vienna, Austria), **11** (Schloss Schonbrunn, Vienna, Austria), **15** (Kunsthistorisches Museum, Vienna, Austria), **18** (Chateau de Versailles/Giraudon/Lauros), **19** (Kunsthistorisches Museum, Vienna, Austria), **20** (British Museum), **21** (Chateau de Versailles/Giraudon), **23** (Musee Antoine Lecuyer, Saint-Quentin, France), **24** (Nationalmuseum, Stockholm, Sweden), **28** (Chateau de Versailles/Giraudon), **30** (Chateau de Versailles), **35** (Musee Conde, Chatilly, France/Giraudon/Lauros), **36** (Musee de la Ville de Paris, Musee Carnavalet, Paris, France/Lauros/Giraudon), **38** (Musee de la Revolution Francaise, Vizille, France), **39** (Bibliotheque Nationale, Paris, France/Lauros/Giraudon), **41** (Chateau de Versailles/Giraudon/Lauros); ©Photolibrary (Juniors Bildarchiv) **p. 17**.

Cover photograph of reproduced with permission of © The Bridgeman Art Library (Giraudon/ Lauros/ Chateau de Versailles, France).

The publishers would like to thank Nancy Harris for her assistance in the preparation of this book.

Every effort has been made to contact copyright holders of any material reproduced in this book. Any omissions will be rectified in subsequent printings if notice is given to the publisher.

Disclaimer
All the Internet addresses (URLs) given in this book were valid at the time of going to press. However, due to the dynamic nature of the Internet, some addresses may have changed, or sites may have changed or ceased to exist since publication. While the author and publisher regret any inconvenience this may cause readers, no responsibility for any such changes can be accepted by either the author or the publisher.

Contents

Marie Antoinette, Queen of France 4
Antoine of Austria 6
Wedding Plans 10
Moving to France 14
The Young Queen 20
The Troubles Begin .26
Revolution! 32
Death of a Queen 38
Timelines 42
Want to Know More? 44
Glossary 46
Index 48

> Some words are shown in bold, **like this**. You can find out what they mean by looking in the glossary.

Marie Antoinette, Queen of France

Marie Antoinette was queen of France from 1774 to 1792. This was a very dramatic time in France. During her **reign**, the French people turned against their king and queen. They had a violent **rebellion**, which was later known as the French Revolution.

This is a portrait of Marie Antoinette when she was 28 years old.

The French Revolution

The French Revolution lasted from 1789 to 1799. It was a time of chaos in France, when the poor turned against the rich. Thousands of French **nobles** died, and the king and queen were both put to death.

This map shows Europe in 1770.

A life of contrasts

Queen Marie Antoinette was put to death by the French people when she was 37 years old. In her short life, she experienced many changes. She began her life in Austria. Then, when she was 14 years old, she traveled to France and never returned to Austria again.

For nearly 20 years, Queen Marie Antoinette lived in a beautiful French royal palace, but she spent the last years of her life in prison. When she first became queen, she was loved by the French people. At the end of her reign, she was hated and sent to her death.

Villain or victim?

Today, people disagree about Queen Marie Antoinette. Some believe she was a spoiled and thoughtless woman. They say the French people were right to hate her. Many others see her in a different way. They believe she was a helpless **victim**, and they believe she did not deserve her punishment.

Antoine of Austria

On November 2, 1755, a baby girl was born in the Austrian royal palace. She was the eighth daughter of the joint rulers of Austria, Emperor Francis I and his wife, Empress Maria Teresa. The baby was named Maria Antonia Josepha Joanna, but she was always known as "Antoine." Fourteen years later, when Antoine moved to France, her name was changed to Marie Antoinette.

Emperor Francis loved to have fun. His daughter Antoine took after him.

Family life

The emperor and empress both loved children, and they had a very large family. By the time Antoine was born, they already had seven daughters and three sons. Antoine was the second youngest in the royal family. After she was born, her parents had one more boy.

Three palaces

When Antoine was growing up, she had three amazing homes. In winter, the royal family lived in the Hofburg Palace, in the center of the city of Vienna. In summer, they moved to the Schönbrunn Palace to escape from the heat and noise of the city. The palace was 5 miles (8 kilometers) outside of Vienna.

Antoine's favorite family home was the Laxenburg Palace. It was smaller than her other homes and farther from Vienna. This was where the family went to relax on their own. At Laxenburg, they could enjoy themselves without all the lords and ladies who usually took part in the life of the royal **court**.

Empress Maria Teresa was more serious than her husband. She felt she had a duty to rule well.

Empress Maria Teresa was a loving parent, but she was also very strict. She expected her children to obey her without question. The year after Antoine was born, Maria Teresa said about her children:

"They are born to obey and must learn to do so."

Living in style

In the Austrian palaces, all of the royal children had a complete set of rooms of their own. They also had their own personal servants to help them dress and to provide them with everything they needed.

Lessons at home

The Austrian royal children had all their lessons at home. A **governess** taught them reading and writing. Music, singing, and dancing masters also came to the palaces to teach the royal children.

The famous composer Mozart used to play at the Austrian court when he was a boy.

Antoine was a poor student at reading and writing. Even as an adult, she still made messy inkblots when she wrote. But she adored music and was naturally graceful at dancing. She was also a talented musician, and she played the harp and the harpsichord with great skill.

Privilege and poverty
The young Antoine lived a life of great **privilege**. For her, it was normal to live in vast palaces and to be waited on by servants. Meanwhile, most people in Austria were extremely poor. Many of them did not have enough to eat, and some even died from **starvation**.

Fun and games
All the royal children had to spend long hours at the royal court, listening to the adults and being very well-behaved. But they also had the chance to have fun. In winter, they glided over the snow in toboggans shaped like swans. In summer, they went riding on horseback in the royal forests.

The Schönbrunn Palace had a private zoo in the gardens.

Wedding Plans

When Antoine was nine years old, life in the royal palaces changed dramatically. Emperor Francis died suddenly. Antoine was especially close to her father, and so she was heartbroken.

Empress Maria Teresa never recovered from her husband's death. She dressed in black for the rest of her life, and she became even more serious and stern. She kept very busy ruling her lands, but also found the time to choose suitable partners for her children to marry.

Maria Teresa is shown here with her sons. She is wearing black, in mourning for her dead husband.

Many marriages

Maria Teresa's aim was to marry her children to the rulers of powerful countries. This was an excellent way of keeping friends with other countries. At this time, it was very common for a royal child to marry at a young age and to go to live in a different country.

By the time Antoine was 12 years old, most of her brothers and sisters had married kings and queens. Now it was time for her mother to find three powerful rulers to marry Josephina, Charlotte, and Antoine.

Arranged marriages
In the 1700s, wealthy people did not usually marry for love. Instead, most marriages were arranged by the parents of the bride and groom. Wealthy parents tried to find rich and powerful partners for their children.

Josephina and Charlotte

In 1767, Maria Teresa arranged for Josephina to marry the king of Naples, a kingdom in southern Italy. Then, just before the marriage took place, Josephina caught a disease, called **smallpox**, and within a few days she was dead. Maria Teresa was very sad, but she took rapid action. She informed the king that she had two more daughters who could marry him. The king selected Charlotte, who traveled to Naples in the place of her dead sister.

This portrait shows Archduchess Charlotte, Antoine's favorite sister.

Time to change

After Charlotte left, Antoine was the only daughter left at home. She was lonely without her sisters, but she kept busy, preparing to be a royal wife.

In the 1700s, a royal husband expected his wife to be elegant and well-dressed. She had to have perfect manners and ladylike skills, such as dancing and playing the harp. Most men did not want their wife to be too clever, though all royal wives had to be able to read and write easily.

Getting ready

Antoine had metal bands fixed onto her teeth to straighten them. She also learned to pluck some hair from her forehead, to make her hairline perfectly straight. Empress Maria Teresa was shocked at her daughter's poor reading and writing skills, so Antoine was given extra lessons.

A husband for Antoine

By the time Antoine was 13 years old, her mother had found her a husband. He was the 14-year-old French prince, Louis Auguste.

Maria Teresa chose Louis Auguste because he was the **heir** to the French throne, and would be the future ruler of France. If her daughter became queen of France, Maria Teresa could feel confident that France would stay friends with Austria.

Portrait of a prince

There were no photographs in the 18th century, so Antoine had to rely on a painted portrait to see what her future husband looked like. When the painting arrived from France, she was shocked. It showed a boy plowing a field and dressed like a farmer! Later, the French explained that it was the fashion in their country to paint pictures of wealthy people pretending to be **peasants**.

Antoine was only 13 years old when her marriage was arranged.

Moving to France

Once the marriage had been agreed upon by the two royal families, Antoine had to prepare herself for many changes. The French royal family expected her to forget her Austrian ways and become as French as possible. She even had to give up her old name. As soon as she entered France, she would be known as Marie Antoinette.

Preparing for France

In the months before her wedding, Antoine started learning French. She also studied the history of France. Meanwhile, there was more work to be done on her looks. A French hairdresser traveled to Vienna to work on Antoine's hair. All her measurements were taken, so new clothes could be made for her in France, following the latest Paris fashions.

Leaving Austria

At last, Antoine was ready to travel to France. She was very sad to say goodbye to her mother, but Maria Teresa reminded her daughter of her **duty** to be brave.

Empress Maria Teresa gave this advice to Antoine just before she left for France.

"Do so much good to the French people that they can say that I have sent them an angel."

Antoine left Vienna in a grand **procession** of 57 carriages. It took two and half weeks to travel across the Austrian Empire to the border with France, and crowds cheered Antoine all the way. Eventually, the procession arrived at Strasbourg, on the French border.

As Antoine approached the border, she saw a small wooden building. This was the place where she would cross into France. The building stood half in Austria and half in France. As Antoine stepped inside, she knew she was leaving her old life forever.

This portrait shows Marie Antoinette around the time of her marriage.

Becoming Marie Antoinette

Inside the building were two matching rooms, one in Austria, and the other in France. An Austrian **noble** accompanied Antoine to the entrance of the French room. There she was welcomed by her French **ladies-in-waiting**, who called her by her new name of Marie Antoinette.

Once Marie Antoinette was inside the French room, she was dressed in her new French clothes. As she stepped out onto French soil, she became a French princess.

Meeting Louis Auguste

After she crossed the border, Marie Antoinette still had to travel another 250 miles (402 kilometers) to reach Paris. There, King Louis XV and his grandson and **heir**, Prince Louis Auguste, were waiting for her. The king gave Marie Antoinette a warm welcome, but Louis Auguste hardly looked at her.

This is Louis Auguste around the time of his marriage.

An unlucky prince

Louis Auguste was painfully shy and lacking in confidence. When he was a little boy, his parents had **neglected** him and concentrated on his older brother. Then, when Louis was seven years old, his brother died after a long illness, and his parents were heartbroken. They often told Louis that he could never be as good as his dead brother.

When Louis Auguste was 11 years old, his father died, and so Louis became the heir to the French throne. Nobody could imagine how this shy boy could ever be the king of France.

Marie Antionette's pet was a long-haired shih-tzu, like the dog in this photo.

Losing a pet
When Marie Antoinette entered the building on the French border, she carried her little dog. But the French ladies-in-waiting would not allow her to keep her pet. The young princess was very distressed, so it was agreed that the dog would later be sent to her in France.

A royal marriage

Three days after they met, Marie Antoinette and Louis Auguste were married. Marie Antoinette wore a white dress with a very wide skirt, and she was weighed down with precious jewelry.

Life in the palace

After the wedding, the prince and princess lived in the royal palace at Versailles. Marie Antoinette had ladies-in-waiting to do everything for her. They helped her in and out of bed, and even dressed and undressed her.

At Versailles, Marie Antoinette had to get used to being watched. The public was allowed into many parts of the palace, and large crowds gathered to stare at the new princess. The royal couple even had to eat most of their meals in public. Marie Antoinette hated this experience and ate almost nothing. Life at Versailles felt very different from her childhood in the Austrian palaces.

The Palace of Versailles is about 12 miles (19 kilometers) west of Paris.

An odd couple

Louis continued to be very shy with his wife. He preferred to go hunting whenever he could. He also enjoyed reading and making mechanical locks. Marie Antoinette made friends with some noble ladies and spent most of her time gossiping.

This painting shows Marie Antoinette and her husband being visited by her brother.

French society

At the time that Marie Antoinette moved to France, there were three main classes in French society. The royal family and the members of the **aristocracy** lived a life of incredible luxury and paid no **taxes**. The **middle classes** (for example, merchants and lawyers) lived in comfortable houses, but they had to pay heavy taxes to support the rich. The lower classes were mainly **peasants** working on the land. They had very hard lives and little to eat. Even though the peasants were desperately poor, they still had to pay taxes.

The Young Queen

In 1774, King Louis XV died from **smallpox**. Prince Louis Auguste was 20 years old and Marie Antoinette was 18. When they heard the news, the young couple dropped to their knees. They prayed to God for help because they felt they were "too young to rule."

A new king and queen

A few days later, Louis Auguste became King Louis XVI (Louis 16th), and Marie Antoinette became queen of France. After their **coronation**, the new king and queen were welcomed by cheering crowds. The people of France had grown tired of their old king and were delighted by the sight of their elegant young queen.

Medallions were made to celebrate the coronation of King Louis XVI and Queen Marie Antoinette.

This painting shows rich and poor people in France in the 1700s.

Hunger in France

At the time that the new king was crowned, there had been a very bad **harvest**, and many people in France were starving. On the way to her coronation, Marie Antoinette saw many desperate people in the streets. She felt very sorry for her people, and wished to do her best to help them.

After the coronation, Queen Marie Antoinette wrote to her mother, "It is quite certain that in seeing the people who treat us so well despite their own misfortune, we are more **obliged** than ever to work hard for their happiness."

Famous words

There is a famous story that is often told about Marie Antoinette. According to the story, the queen saw some people begging for bread. Instead of giving them something to eat, she is supposed to have said, "Let them eat cake." In fact, there is no record that Marie Antoinette ever said these words. People in France had told the same story about another royal princess 100 years before.

Wasting money

Once she was queen, Marie Antoinette settled down to enjoy a life of great **extravagance**. She spent a fortune on clothes and jewelry, and she loved to hold parties and **gamble** with her friends.

Later, people blamed Queen Marie Antoinette for wasting money, but everyone around her was extravagant. All the French **nobles** spent vast amounts of money on themselves.

Kind but thoughtless

Marie Antoinette was kind and tenderhearted. She hated to see people suffer and she gave money to poor families. But she made no effort to understand the problems of the poor. Whenever anyone tried to talk to her about serious topics, she changed the subject. She insisted that everyone around her should only talk about happy things.

Stories and rumors

At Versailles, the queen surrounded herself with her favorites. In particular, she was very close to her dressmaker and her hairdresser. Some people at court **resented** the fact that the queen's favorites were given such good treatment. Gradually, the queen began to make some powerful enemies.

Marie Antoinette's enemies spread many stories and **rumors** about her. They said she stayed out gambling all night and had secret meetings with men. They also said she was a bad wife, and they blamed her for the fact that the royal couple had not produced an **heir** to the throne.

Marie Antoinette is famous for her hairstyle, called a "pouf."

High hair

The queen's enemies loved to make fun of her hairstyle, known as a pouf. In this extreme style, the hair is sprinkled with powder to make it stiff and white, and then piled up very high over pads. Marie Antoinette's poufs were as much as 3 feet (1 meter) high. They were decorated with feathers, jewels, and ornaments.

This portrait shows Marie Antoinette with her children in the park of the Trianon.

A child at last

In 1778, after eight years of marriage, Queen Marie Antoinette finally had a child. She gave birth to a little girl named Marie Thérèse, after the baby's Austrian grandmother. Marie Antoinette was delighted with her baby daughter, but King Louis had hoped for a son. At that time, people believed that men made stronger rulers than women, so the king needed a son to be his heir.

A growing family

Over the next nine years, Marie Antoinette had three more children. In 1781, she gave birth to a son, who was named Louis Joseph. Now King Louis had an heir at last, and he was delighted. Then four years later, a second son, Louis Charles, was born. The following year, the queen had another daughter, who was named Sophie Béatrix.

A personal palace

Marie Antoinette loved her children passionately. Whenever she could, she stayed with them in her personal palace, called Le Petit Trianon. This was a miniature palace in the grounds of Versailles that the king had given her as a present. Queen Marie Antoinette and her children treated Le Petit Trianon like a giant playhouse.

Watching the birth

When the queen's first child was born, the birth was watched by a large number of **courtiers**. Marie Antoinette was very upset by this experience and she refused to give birth in public again. The reason for this ancient **custom** was to make sure that the queen was really giving birth. In the past, some queens had been so desperate for an heir that they had **smuggled** a baby into their bedroom and pretended the baby was their own.

This is the Petit Trianon, where Marie Antoinette sometimes stayed with her children.

The Troubles Begin

As Marie Antoinette approached the age of 30, she became less **extravagant** than before, but that did not mean she stopped spending money. While her children were still very young, the queen began work on a grand plan. She created her own village in the grounds of Versailles.

This portrait shows Marie Antoinette dressed in peasant clothing.

A pretend village

Marie Antoinette's pretend village was known as Le Hameau. It was a group of pretty cottages surrounded by beautiful countryside. The queen loved to spend time there with her children, dressing very simply and playing at village life.

In France at that time it was very fashionable to dress in **peasants'** clothes and pretend to live a simple country life. Meanwhile, many real country dwellers in France were starving. The French people saw their queen's play-acting as a sign of how little she understood their suffering.

A necklace for the queen?

In 1785, a **noblewoman** at court played a cruel trick on Marie Antoinette. She gave orders for an incredibly expensive diamond necklace to be made and claimed it had been ordered for the queen. The "diamond necklace affair" became a famous scandal, and people blamed the queen for her extravagance. The noblewoman was eventually sent to prison. But the French people did not change their opinion of Marie Antoinette.

Problems of the poor

While Marie Antoinette was queen, the ordinary people of France were becoming poorer. The **population** of France was growing fast. There were also some very bad **harvests**, which led to serious shortages of grain for bread. Many people were starving and homeless. There were not enough jobs for everyone, and people suffered from many diseases.

This painting of people in rural France showed how poor people had become in the 1700s.

Death in the family

Around the time of the diamond necklace affair, Marie Antoinette had to cope with some very sad events. In 1787, her baby daughter, Sophie, died from a childhood illness, just before her first birthday. Not long after this, the royal doctor told her that her oldest son, Louis Joseph, was dying from a serious lung disease. Marie Antoinette spent all the time she could caring for her son.

This painting illustrates the death of Marie Antoinette's baby daughter, Sophie. The baby was originally shown in her cradle, but after she died the artist had to paint her out of the picture.

Money troubles

At this difficult time, the royal family also faced serious money problems. King Louis had spent a fortune at Versailles. He had also been involved in some expensive wars abroad. Now he badly needed more money. He decided that he must ask the French people to pay more **taxes**.

Talking to the people

In order to raise more taxes, Louis needed to ask permission from the **Estates General**. This was a group of men who represented the French people. So, in May 1789 he called a meeting of the Estates General.

Before this meeting, the French kings had ignored the Estates General for 175 years. Many members of the Estates General were furious that their views had been ignored for so long. They were also very angry about the way that France was run. Now at last they had the chance to speak out.

Power to the people

The Estates General included some members of the French **middle classes**. These people also represented the French peasants. Usually the peasants had no chance to make their views known. They were determined to tell King Louis just how desperate and angry they were.

The French people were angry because King Louis spent so much money on luxuries.

Protest and pain

As soon as the Estates General met, they began to protest. They demanded major changes in the way that France was run. This was very worrying for King Louis, but he had other problems to deal with.

On June 4, 1789, Prince Louis Joseph died and his younger brother became the new **heir**. The king and queen were desperately sad about their dead son. To make things even worse, Marie Antoinette's enemies at court spread **rumors** that she had poisoned Louis Joseph.

A dangerous situation

During the month of June, the situation in France became very dangerous. A group of powerful men began to make plans to take over the government of France. This frightened King Louis, who feared that Paris was in danger.

On July 1, Louis sent some troops to gather outside Paris. Now the people of Paris were afraid that the city would be attacked. They prepared to defend themselves by gathering weapons.

Storming the Bastille

On July 14, a large **mob** of people broke into the Bastille prison, in central Paris. They demanded that the prison guards hand over all their weapons. The guards were powerless to resist, and the mob took over the prison. This dramatic event is known as the storming of the Bastille, and it marks the start of the French Revolution.

Challenging the king

To the people of Paris, the Bastille was a symbol of royal power. The king kept all his enemies locked up in there. When the mob stormed the Bastille, they showed that they were prepared to challenge the king.

This image shows the storming of the Bastille. You can see the crowds rushing through the prison gates.

Revolution!

After the storming of the Bastille, **peasants** all over France attacked the homes of the rich. Meanwhile, people in Paris were running short of food. When they heard that the king and queen were holding grand banquets, an angry **mob** decided to march to Versailles.

A large crowd marched from Paris to Versailles, led by a group of very angry women.

Royal prisoners

On October 5, 1789, a large crowd arrived at the royal palace. They were led by women, shouting **abuse** at the queen. The royal family locked themselves inside the palace, but the following day they were forced to travel to Paris.

Once they reached Paris, the royal family were held as prisoners in the crumbling Palace of the Tuileries. It was a gloomy place, but Marie Antoinette made a great effort to stay calm and cheerful for the sake of her children.

A royal plan

By 1791, the king and queen were sure that the Revolution would destroy France. They planned to escape to a safe place and gather support against the leaders of the Revolution.

In the end, the plan failed. The king was recognized while they tried to escape, and the royal family was forced to return to Paris. Now it was clear to everyone that the king and queen were enemies of the Revolution.

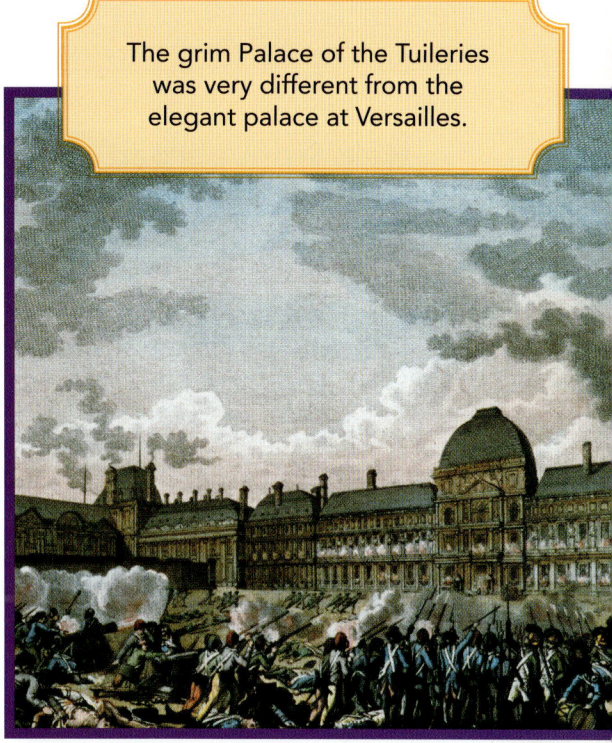

The grim Palace of the Tuileries was very different from the elegant palace at Versailles.

Liberty, Equality, Fraternity

For many people in France, the French Revolution was about **revenge**. They wanted to attack the rich people who had treated them so badly. But some leaders of the Revolution hoped to build a better society. The three things they believed in were Liberty (freedom for all); Equality (equal rights for all); and Fraternity (a sense of brotherhood among all people).

Help from abroad?

After they had failed to escape from Paris, the royal family put all their faith in the other rulers of Europe. They hoped that these powerful leaders could rescue them. But things did not turn out the way they expected.

A threat from Austria

In August 1792, the emperor of Austria gathered an army on the border of France. Then he sent a message to the people of Paris. He threatened to destroy their city if any harm came to the royal family.

The Austrian queen
Many French people hated Marie Antoinette because she was Austrian. They were suspicious of her foreign ways, and they were afraid of the powerful Austrian Empire. The queen's enemies often spread **rumors** about her foreign plots. They said that she was planning to destroy France with members of her Austrian family.

The emperor thought his threat would force the French people to release their king. But it had the opposite result. It made people hate the royal family even more. The Austrian emperor was the nephew of Marie Antoinette, and many people suspected that they had **plotted** together.

When they heard about the Austrian emperor's threat, an angry mob attacked the Tuileries. They charged at the gates with axes and spades, howling for the queen to be put to death.

Emperor Francis II of Austria was the most powerful ruler in Europe.

The end of the monarchy

In September, the leaders of the Revolution passed a law to put an end to the **monarchy**. Now Louis and Marie Antoinette were no longer king and queen, and they could be treated much more harshly. They were moved to a new prison and locked in a tower.

Death of a king

In December 1792, King Louis was given a **trial** and **condemned** to death. A month later he was **beheaded** on the **guillotine**. Before his death he was allowed to say goodbye to his family. The children cried and screamed and refused to be parted from their father, and the queen was heartbroken.

Farewell to Louis Charles

At the time of King Louis's death, his daughter, Marie Thérèse, was 15 years old. His son and heir, Louis Charles, was only seven. For the next six months, they continued to live in the tower with their mother.

Late one night in July, some prison guards came to seize Louis Charles. They imprisoned him in a separate room, but Marie Antoinette could still hear him crying through the walls. After that night, Marie Antoinette never saw her son again. He died in prison two years later. Marie Thérèse was freed from prison when she was 17, and she went on to survive after the Revolution.

This painting shows Marie Antoinette as a prisoner.

A new prison

In August 1893, Marie Antoinette was taken to a new prison. By this time, she was very ill and weak, and she was kept in a room on her own. There was one more plan to help her escape, but it failed.

When the French people heard about the escape plan, they were very angry. The crowd began to call for Marie Antoinette to be put to death.

The guillotine was used to execute thousands of people during the French Revolution.

Many deaths
During the French Revolution, over 18,000 people were put to death. Most of these people were beheaded on the guillotine. The guillotine was a tall wooden frame with a hole, where the **victim** placed his or her neck, and a very sharp iron blade that was pulled down by a rope.

Death of a Queen

Marie Antoinette was ready for death, but first she had to face a **trial**. When she entered the courtroom, everyone was shocked. The last time they had seen her, she had been a beautiful young queen, dressed in the finest clothes. Now she was dressed in very plain clothes and looked like an old woman. In fact Marie Antoinette was only 37, but her sufferings had made her look much older.

At her trial, Marie Antoinette was accused of many crimes against France, and 40 people spoke out against her. At the end of the trial, she was **condemned** to death on the **guillotine**.

At her trial, Marie Antoinette appealed to the mothers of France for mercy.

This painting shows Marie Antoinette by the guillotine, with her hair cropped and her hands bound.

A last journey

On the morning of the **execution**, a guard arrived at Marie Antoinette's cell. He cut her hair short and tied her hands behind her back. Then he forced her into an open cart, known as a tumbril. The journey to the guillotine took over an hour. People lined the streets along the way and mocked the queen as she passed.

A brave death

Marie Antoinette was calm and **dignified** right up until the end of her life. There is a famous story that she even apologized to the **executioner** when she accidentally stood on his foot.

After Marie Antoinette's execution, the crowds cheered loudly. They were delighted that their queen was dead.

As Marie Antoinette approached the guillotine, a priest told her to take courage. She replied:

"Courage? The moment when my troubles are going to end is not the moment when my courage is going to fail me."

After Marie Antoinette

The French Revolution continued for six more years after the queen's death. Then a powerful leader named Napoleon Bonaparte made himself emperor of France. But Napoleon's empire lasted for only nine years.

By 1814, France had a king again. For the next 30 years, the French were ruled by kings. Then there was a second revolution. Today, France is a **republic**—a country without a king or queen.

Changing views

After the French Revolution, Marie Antoinette was still hated in France. Then, gradually, some people began to see her in a different way. They stopped thinking of her as a cruel and thoughtless woman. Instead they saw her as a **victim** who did not have the power to change the way the ruling classes lived in France.

In 1815, the bodies of Marie Antoinette and King Louis were given a royal burial. They were buried in the Cathedral of Saint Denis in Paris, with the other kings and queens of France.

People have different opinions about Marie Antoinette, but there is no doubt that she will be remembered for a long time.

A selfish queen?

Today, a few people still see Marie Antoinette as a selfish person. They believe she just wanted to enjoy herself and did not care if other people suffered. But most people think this picture is wrong. Before the Revolution, Marie Antoinette lived a life of luxury, but she was also a loving mother. In the last years of her life, she suffered greatly, but she remained dignified and brave.

Helping the poor?

Marie Antoinette made some attempts to help the poor people of France. Throughout her **reign**, she gave large sums of money to the poor. She was also very kind to some **peasant** families who lived close to Versailles. But the amounts of money she gave to the poor were a tiny **proportion** of the fortune she spent on herself and her family.

Timelines

Marie Antoinette's Life

1755   Maria Antonia Josepha Joanna is born. She is soon known as "Antoine." Her parents are the emperor and empress of Austria.

1770   Antoine travels to France to marry Prince Louis Auguste.

1774   Louis Auguste becomes King Louis XVI of France. Marie Antoinette becomes queen of France.

1778   Marie Antoinette gives birth to a daughter, Marie Thérèse.

1781   Marie Antoinette has a son, Louis Joseph. He is the **heir** to the French throne.

1785   Marie Antoinette has a second son, Louis Charles.

1786   Marie Antoinette has a second daughter, Sophie Béatrix, who dies the following year.

1789   June: Prince Louis Joseph dies. Louis Charles becomes the heir to the French throne.
July: The Bastille is stormed. The French Revolution begins.
October: The royal family is captured at Versailles and taken to the Tuileries Palace in Paris.

1793   January: King Louis XVI is **executed.**
October: Marie Antoinette is executed .

1795   Prince Louis Charles dies in prison.

1795   Marie Thérèse is freed from prison at age 17.

1799   The French Revolution ends.

1815   Louis XVI and Marie Antoinette are buried with the other kings and queens of France.

World Timeline

1750s The Industrial Revolution begins in Britain.

1762 Catherine the Great becomes empress of Russia.

1770 Captain Cook reaches Australia.

1775 The American Revolutionary War begins in North America.

1776 The Declaration of Independence is signed in North America.

1782 James Watts invents a powerful steam engine.

1789 The French Revolution begins. George Washington becomes the first president of the United States.

1799 Napoleon takes control of France.

Want to Know More?

Books

Lasky, Kathryn. *The Royal Diaries: Marie Antoinette: Princess of Versailles, Austria-France, 1769*. New York: Scholastic, 2000.

Lotz, Nancy and Phillips, Carlene. *Marie Antoinette and the Decline of French Monarchy*. Greensboro, North Carolina: Morgan Reynolds Publishing Inc., 2004.

Macdonald, Fiona. *The World in the Time of Marie Antoinette*. New York: Chelsea House, 2000.

Websites

www.kidspast.com/world-history/0370-french-revolution.php

This website tells the story of the French Revolution, and what happened after it. There are some fun games to play, too.

www.socialstudiesforkids.com/subjects/frenchrevolution.htm

This is a helpful site on the French revolution, with a section on Marie Antoinette. You can even send your friends a Bastille Day card!

http://www.surfnetkids.com/marie_antoinette.htm

Find out if Marie Antoinette really said, "Let them eat cake!"

Places to visit

Denver Art Museum, Denver, Colorado

100 W 14th Avenue Parkway • Denver, CO 80204 • (720) 865-5000

www.denverartmuseum.org

An exhibition called "Artisans and Kings" from the Louvre Museum in Paris, France shows treasures from Marie Antoinette's day.

The Metropolitan Museum of Art, New York

1000 5th Avenue • New York, NY 10028 • (212) 535-7710

www.metmuseum.org

See Marie Antoinette's desk from the palace of Versailles, and many paintings from the French Revolution era.

Glossary

abuse rude or unkind words

aristocracy members of the highest social rank in society

beheaded killed by having your head cut off

condemned forced to suffer something bad

coronation religious service in which a new king or queen is crowned

court people who gather around a ruler, including advisors and servants

courtier someone who is close to a ruler, and is an important figure at the royal court

custom action that has been performed many times in the past, and has become an accepted way to behave

dignified calm and in control

duty things that someone must do or should do

Estates General group of men who represented the French people at the time of the French Revolution. The Estates General was a kind of parliament.

execution officially putting someone to death

executioner person who officially puts someone to death

extravagance spending too much money on things that are not needed

gamble bet money on a game or an event

governess woman who teaches children in their own home

guillotine tall wooden frame with a sliding metal blade, used to behead people

harvest gathering up of crops at the end of the growing season

heir someone who will receive money, land, or a job, when his or her parents die

lady-in-waiting woman who helps to look after a queen

middle class people such as lawyers, shopkeepers, and teachers, who were neither peasants nor members of the aristocracy

mob large and dangerous crowd of people

monarchy kings and queens

neglect fail to look after someone properly

noble member of a very high rank in society. Lords and ladies are nobles.

noblewoman woman who has a high rank in society

obliged feel that you must or should do something

peasant someone who works on the land and is very poor

plot secret plan

population the people who live in a certain place

privilege special advantages given to a person or a group

procession group of people or vehicles moving together in a line

proportion part of something larger

rebellion violent protest against a ruler or government

reign period of time that a king or queen rules for

republic country or state that votes for its ruler and does not have a king or queen

resent feel hurt or angry about something

revenge actions to pay someone back for what they have done

rumor stories that people spread, which are often cruel and not true

smallpox very serious disease in which people develop spots all over the body, and often die

smuggle take something in or out of a place secretly

starvation severe lack of food, which can result in death

taxes money that people have to pay to a government or a ruler

trial examination in a court of someone who has been accused of a crime

victim someone who suffers because of something that is not his or her fault

Index

America 44
American Revolutionary War 44
aristocracy 19
arranged marriages 11, 13
Australia 44
Austria 5, 6-15, 34

Bastille, storming of 31, 42
Cathedral of St Denis 40
Catherine the Great 43
childbirth, public 25
Conciergerie 36, 37
"diamond necklace affair" 27, 28

education, royal 8-9
Estates General 29, 30
extravagance 22, 26, 30

Francis I, Emperor of Austria 6, 10
Francis II, Emperor of Austria 34, 35
French Revolution 4, 31, 32-40, 42, 43, 44

gambling 22
guillotine 36, 37, 38, 39

hairstyles 23
harvests, poor 27
heir to the throne 22, 25, 30
Hofburg Palace 6

Industrial Revolution 43

Josephina 11

ladies-in-waiting 16, 17, 18
Laxenburg Palace 7
le Hameau 26
Le Petit Trianon 24, 25
Liberty, Equality and Fraternity 33
Louis XV of France 16, 20
Louis XVI of France 12, 16-17, 18, 19, 20, 24, 25, 29, 30-1, 36, 43
Louis Charles 36, 42, 43
Louis Joseph 25, 28, 30, 42

Maria Carolina (Charlotte) 11
Maria Teresa, Empress of Austria 6, 7, 10-11, 12, 14
Marie Antoinette
 birth and early life 5, 6-9, 10, 11-12
 character and abilities 5, 9, 12, 21, 22, 40, 41
 children 24-5, 28, 36
 coronation 20, 42
 enemies of 22, 30, 34, 38
 escape plans 33, 37
 execution 5, 39, 43
 extravagance 22, 26
 hairstyles 23
 imprisonment 33, 34, 35, 36, 37
 marriage 12, 14-18
 portraits 4, 13, 15, 19, 20, 23, 24, 26, 28, 36, 38, 39, 41
 trial 38
Marie Thérèse 24, 36, 42, 43
middle classes 19, 29
Mozart, Wolfgang Amadeus 8

Naples 11
Napoleon Bonaparte 40, 43

Paris 16, 31
peasants 12, 19, 26, 32, 41
pouf hairstyles 23
poverty 9, 19, 21, 26, 27, 41

republic 40

Schönbrunn Palace 6, 9
shih-tzu 17
smallpox 11, 20, 44
social classes 19
Sophie Beatrix 25, 28, 42
starvation 9, 21, 26, 27
steam engines 44
Strasbourg 15

taxes 19, 29
Tuileries 33, 34, 42, 43
tumbrils 39

Versailles 18, 22, 25, 26, 29, 32-3, 41
Vienna 6, 15

Washington, George 43
Watts, James 43